MAJE

SOUTH

AFRICA

D0634008

MAJESTIC
SOUTH
AFRICA

a photographic celebration
of stunning natural beauty

wilf nussey

southwater

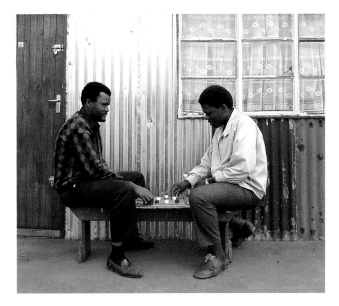

This edition is published by Southwater

Southwater is an imprint of Anness Publishing Ltd
Hermes House, 88–89 Blackfriars Road, London SE1 8HA
tel. 020 7401 2077; fax 020 7633 9499
www.southwaterbooks.com; info@anness.com

© Anness Publishing Ltd 1997, 2005

UK agent: The Manning Partnership Ltd,
6 The Old Dairy, Melcombe Road, Bath BA2 3LR;
tel. 01225 478444; fax 01225 478440;
sales@manning-partnership.co.uk

UK distributor: Grantham Book Services Ltd,
Isaac Newton Way, Alma Park Industrial Estate,
Grantham, Lincs NG31 9SD;
tel. 01476 541080; fax 01476 541061;
orders@gbs.tbs-ltd.co.uk

North American agent/distributor: National Book Network, 4501
Forbes Boulevard, Suite 200,
Lanham, MD 20706;
tel. 301 459 3366; fax 301 429 5746;
www.nbnbooks.com

Australian agent/distributor: Pan Macmillan Australia,
Level 18, St Martins Tower, 31 Market St, Sydney,
NSW 2000;
tel. 1300 135 113; fax 1300 135 103;
customer.service@macmillan.com.au

New Zealand agent/distributor: David Bateman Ltd,
30 Tarndale Grove, Off Bush Road,
Albany, Auckland;
tel. (09) 415 7664; fax (09) 415 8892

All rights reserved. No part of this publication may be reproduced,
stored in a retrieval system, or transmitted in any way or by any means,
electronic, mechanical, photocopying, recording or otherwise, without
the prior written permission of the copyright holder.

A CIP catalogue record for this book is available from the British Library.

10 9 8 7 6 5 4 3 2 1

Contents

Page 1: *Top*: Dried bokkems or harders, Cape herrings, are a staple among West Coast fisherfolk. *Centre*: Dried mopane worms, caterpillars of an emperor moth, are an African delicacy. *Bottom*: Guests at the luxury Mala Mala private reserve in Mpumalanga Province study snoozing lions. Page 2: *Top left*: Young elephant at play in the Addo Elephant National Park, Eastern Cape. *Top right*: Long-vanished Bushmen painted stylized animals on rock overhangs like this one in KwaZulu/Natal. *Centre left*: A flock of lesser flamingos feeding in shallow water near Kimberley, Northern Cape. *Centre right*: A student takes a rubbing from one of thousands of mysterious rock engravings in the Free State. *Bottom left*: The tiny lesser bushbaby of the sub-tropics has huge eyes for hunting insects by night. *Bottom right*: Much of the old Kimberley of the 1880s diamond days has been beautifully restored. Page 3: *Top*: The bright colours and smiles of the new South Africa at a roadside stall. *Centre*: A rustic farm shed on the Millstream trout farm in Mpumalanga's high country. *Bottom*: An exuberant display of pumpkins and calabashes of all kinds at a Western Cape roadside shop. Page 4: *Top*: Shantytown dwellers pass the time playing African chequers with bottletops. *Centre*: Hang-gliders like to launch from this high seaside dune in the Eastern Cape. *Bottom*: A tranquil moment on a misty morning in Mpumalanga. Opposite page: *Top*: Clear streams wind through the magnificent Woodbush State Forest near Tzaneen in Northern Province. *Centre*: The lights of Hillbrow in central Johannesburg shine like a basket of jewels at sunset. *Bottom*: The Drakensberg's green foothills in the Eastern Cape are ideal for sheep farming.

Introduction

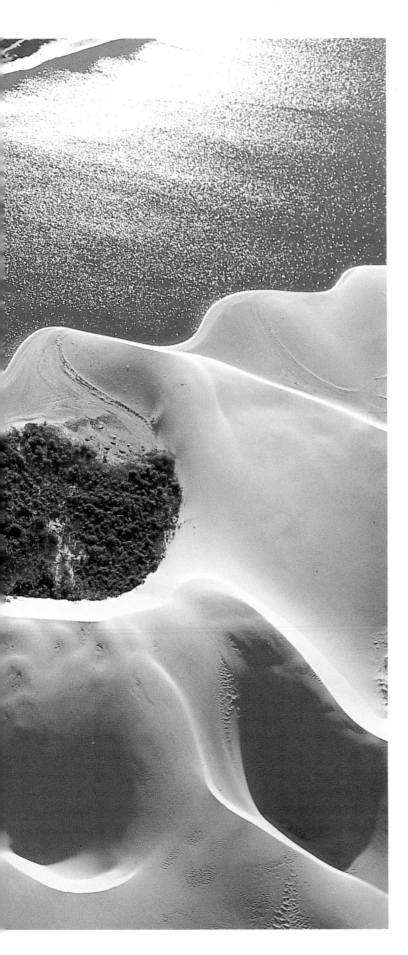

Introduction

By abandoning apartheid in 1990 and rejoining the world, South Africa has reopened the way to a land of warmth and magnificence half forgotten by outsiders during the lonely decades when it was internationally disgraced; quarantined behind barriers of sanctions and censure.

Since then the flow of visitors has grown almost four-fold to nearly four million a year, about a quarter of them tourists, and its cities' bright lights and opportunities have lured between two and eleven million illegal immigrants, most of them African. They have found a vibrant new society in an astonishingly beautiful environment.

The country, covering 1,219,090 square kilometres (470,690 square miles) at Africa's southern tip – slightly smaller than Mexico, twice as big as France – shares most of the continent's characteristics plus facets uniquely its own. It spans about 2,000 kilometres (1,250 miles) from the Limpopo River in the north to Cape Agulhas in the south and about 1,500 kilometres (930 miles) at its widest between the Indian and Atlantic Oceans.

The oceans meet at the southernmost part of its 3,000 kilometre (1,865 mile) coastline – the Western Cape, place of mountainous seas and eternal home of the legendary Flying Dutchman. Beyond, 5,000 kilometres (3,000 miles) of empty ocean stretch south to Antarctica.

The country has two principal regions. One is the long narrow lowland in the east between the Indian Ocean and the 3,376 metre (11,075 foot) ramparts of the Great Drakensberg ("Dragon Mountains") Escarpment, source of great rivers. This mountainous area is seamed by rivers, speckled with forests and fringed by lagoons, coral and brilliant beaches – countryside made lush by the warmth that the south-flowing Agulhas Current brings from the

Left: The ancient sand dunes at the mouth of the Gamtoos River in the Eastern Cape are rich in hidden life and also conceal stone flakes and other artefacts left by vanished Strandloper ("Beachcomber") Bushmen.

Above: A fine view of the Lisbon Falls in the Drakensberg Escarpment with the river in normal flow. When it floods the falls can be hazardous.

equatorial tropics. Here live one-fifth of the people, most of them the renowned Zulus.

The other region is a giant plateau sloping gradually westwards from the high rim of the Drakensberg, growing increasingly arid through the Kalahari and Karoo semi-deserts until it becomes pure desert at the Atlantic coast, washed by icy water brought north from the Antarctic by the Benguela Current.

Within these zones are many sub-regions, each with its own personality. Some are stunningly beautiful, others bleak, all fascinating. They contain ranges of mountains, vast dry plains studded with strange hills, and torrid bushveld intersected by few rivers. Most of the land is sparsely populated, except around cities and towns. The climate is mild and gentle everywhere except in some regional extremes, and sunshine averages eight hours a day.

Scattered over 16 national parks, hundreds of provincial and private reserves, and farms everywhere is an unsurpassed diversity of wildlife – all accessible. South Africa contains abundant populations of most species of African creatures, from elephants to insects, and is the last resort for some, such as the endangered rhino. It also has species unique to southern Africa, like the springbok and gemsbok. There are more than 22,000 kinds of plants – many in two of the world's richest flower kingdoms, nearly 900 species of birds, more than 300 of mammals, nearly 400 of reptiles and roughly 80,000 species of insects and still counting.

Of the original inhabitants whom Portuguese explorers encountered five centuries ago and the first Dutch settlers traded with on their arrival in 1652, the Khoi or Hottentot people were absorbed by the newcomers and the San, the diminutive Bushmen, retreated into the deserts. Over the decades, whites moving inland encountered Xhosa- and Bantu-speaking tribes who had begun to move slowly south from middle Africa between 1,200 and 600 years ago. Their history is scarred by conflicts.

Colonial governments, then independent Afrikaner republics, then the unified South Africa created in 1912, consistently subdued and dominated the majority blacks, from 1948 through the inhuman system of apartheid. The apartheid regime admitted failure in 1990 and in 1994 blacks took their rightful place in a government led by Nelson Mandela, following the first election in which all South Africans were able to take part. But not even apartheid could prevent inter-dependence, and over more than three centuries the white, black and coloured populations evolved the remarkable co-existence which makes possible the present "Rainbow Nation".

South Africa's estimated population of more than 41 million is a vivacious mix of 31 million blacks in nine ethnic groups, about 5.2 million whites (English and Afrikaans), just over one million Asians and 3.5 million people whose blood is a cocktail of the others. They span a spectrum of cultures from Iron Age to modern and East to West, speak more than eleven languages and rub shoulders equally in the worlds of politics, religion, sport and business.

Once based almost entirely on gold, diamonds and farming, South Africa's economy is now so far diversified that manufacturing is the biggest contributor to a gross domestic product which is around 100 billion US dollars (nearly 647 billion rand or around £560 billion), four times

that of its Southern African neighbours and one-quarter of that of the whole African continent. Its output is between one-third and a half of Africa's total.

But nearly half the population, which has grown about tenfold since 1900, still lives in backward rural areas with poor services. Millions have flooded to overcrowded urban slums, wealth is unevenly spread, productivity has waned, standards of education are low, crime is high and it will take generations to right the imbalances.

That is the prime objective of today's government. To facilitate administration the former four provinces have been rearranged into nine, each with its own government and representatives in the central government, whose legislative capital is Cape Town, judicial capital Bloemfontein and administrative capital Pretoria.

In the following pages we take you on a pictorial tour of life and times in modern-day South Africa.

Everlastings bloom on the high cold slopes of the Golden Gate Highlands National Park in the Free State.

Northern Province and Mpumalanga

These provinces in the north and north-east share South Africa's greatest store of wild animals amid majestic scenery. The famous Kruger National Park – 21,539 square kilometres (8,316 square miles) of hot lowland running for 380 kilometres (235 miles) along the Mozambique border – is divided about equally between them.

Among the world's largest and most diverse parks, its 36 camps give some 800,000 people a year extraordinary close-ups of elephant, lion, rhino, buffalo, leopard, hippo, crocodile, many kinds of buck, over 500 raptor and other bird species, some 50,000 kinds of insects and 2,000 species of plants. One area of the park is second only to the Western Cape for its wealth of wild flowers.

But Northern's 123,910 square kilometres (47,840 square miles) and Mpumalanga's 79,490 (30,690) encompass much more. The Drakensberg Escarpment winds through both, an awesome palisade of cliffs and peaks towering up to 1,000 metres (3,280 feet) above the lowlands. On top is high cold plateau with maize fields and fine trout-fishing; below is hot bushy sub-tropics with crops like tea, coffee, citrus, mangoes, macadamias, pecans, papayas and sugar; between is a paradise of mountain and canyon, bedecked with riotous forest and bejewelled with breathtaking waterfalls and lakes.

Fine metalled roads through spectacular passes link the many towns and villages, including 19th-century gold-rush settlements like picturesque Pilgrim's Rest, and scores of provincial and private game reserves, spas and lodges with liquidly musical names such as Ulusaba, Cybele, Matumi, Ngala, Mala Mala, Londolozi, Sabi Sabi and Inyati. Some are ultra-luxurious and very expensive.

Left: The remote Luvuvhu Valley in the north of the Kruger National Park has a huge range of plants that might equal that of the famed Cape floral kingdom. Dinosaur fossils have been found in this hot tropical region – habitat of a great many wild animals and birds – and also the ruins of ancient African settlements.

Northern (population 5.4 million, mainly Pedi and Tsonga) boasts rare sights like the landscape near Messina of huge baobab trees up to 2,000 years old, the thick forest of prehistoric cycads ruled by the revered rainmaker queen, Modjadji, and the mysterious mountains and sacred lakes of the Venda people. A superb new national park, Marakele, covers a plateau on a sandstone massif north of the iron-mining centre of Thabazimbi. In the north-west, adjoining Botswana and Zimbabwe, the land is wild and raw, home to trophy-hunting game ranches.

Mpumalanga ("Where the Sun Rises", population 3 million, mainly Swazi, Zulu and Pedi) had great gold rushes in the late 1800s and several mines still operate. Some are in what is thought to be the largest volcanic crater on earth, the huge, ancient De Kaap Valley at Barberton, where the world's oldest rocks and life forms were discovered.

One of the most popular ways of seeing this region's many facets is on foot along a wide skein of hiking trails and, in the Kruger National Park, along walking trails where one routinely comes face to face with lion, elephant and other animals – with armed rangers standing by.

Below: Burchell's zebra are one of the commonest species in the Kruger National Park and are a favourite food of lions. Some, like several in this group enjoying an afternoon drink at a lily-edged waterhole, have shadow stripes between the bold black and white.

Bottom left: A common flap-neck chameleon appears to be carrying its supper on its back as it gives a ride to a grasshopper. Chameleons tend to court disaster, crossing roads slowly, but this one is reasonably safe in the Kruger National Park, where animals have right of way.

Bottom right: The giraffe's great height enables it to browse where no other animals can reach and its extremely tough tongue and lips effortlessly strip the thorniest branches.

A forest of yellow-stemmed fever trees at Pafuri in the north of the Kruger National Park. Because they grow in damp areas they were thought to be linked to malaria and were avoided by campers, until the mosquito, which breeds in these damp places, was found to be the culprit.

Top: The white rhino, saved from extinction in South Africa. It is not white – the word is a corruption of the Dutch *wyde*, "wide", describing its mouth.

Above: Egrets take to their perches for the night as the sun sets over the Rooibosrand dam in the Kruger National Park.

Right: A rising full moon adds to the mystique of a burly baobab tree. They can live for thousands of years; elephants eat the bark, the fruit makes a refreshing drink for people and animals, many small creatures live in their branches and holes, and hollow baobabs have been variously used as homes, storage sheds and pubs. African legend says God kicked them out of heaven and they landed head first with their roots in the air.

Left: Like people, chacma baboons enjoy their midday nap, and this one in the Kruger National Park has chosen a patch of warm earth to drop off into a long, peaceful sleep. Baboons are highly social animals and there are always several of them on sentry duty while the rest of the troop eat, play or rest.

Below left: Spotted hyenas are also social animals and live and hunt in close-knit packs. The dark colour of the cub shows that it was born very recently.

Below: Young elephant bulls enjoy jousting and it is their way of learning to fight, as these two are doing in the Kruger National Park. They seldom hurt each other except when they are challenging for herd dominance, when they can kill.

Opposite above: Among the Kruger National Park's greatest attractions are its trail camps where people can walk in the bush with armed rangers. Here a group rests on a hilltop on the Bushman Trail, where many Bushman paintings can be seen.

Opposite below left: Masorini is an accurate reconstruction by archaeologists of an African iron-smelters' village that existed in the Kruger National Park nearly 200 years ago.

Opposite below right: These old walls, found recently in the Kruger National Park and rebuilt by archaeologists, are part of Thulamela, a town that thrived four to five centuries ago as a southern outpost of the Kingdom of Monomatapa. Old artefacts have been found during excavations here.

Northern Province and Mpumalanga

Above: The untidy nests of buffalo weavers festoon dead trees standing in the Kruger National Park's lakes and dams, where they are safe from climbing predators.

Left: Placid here but a swollen torrent when good rains fall in its catchment, the nearby Drakensberg Mountains, the Sabie River is one of the Kruger National Park's major arteries, supporting large numbers of hippo, crocodile, terrapin, fish, fish eagles, elephants, buffalo and other animals over a wide area.

Above: A light haze floats above the quiet waters of the Sabie River as the late afternoon sun turns its surface to gold, silhouetting reeds and grass.

Left: Like all Kruger National Park residents, lions ignore vehicles and casually stop traffic to exercise their right of way. They react instantly, however, when people are foolish enough to get out of their cars.

Opposite: The Drakensberg Escarpment in Mpumalanga Province has hundreds of scenic waterfalls, many of which are easily accessible. This one is the Bridal Veil Falls in indigenous forest in the Sabie district.

Above: On its way down from the top of the Drakensberg Escarpment, the Blyde ("Joyous") River has carved fantastic holes, caves and gulleys through sandstone and dolomite, hideout of many trout.

Right: Over the millennia the Blyde River cut a huge canyon on its way to the Lowveld. Now a reserve, this scenic panorama, 700 metres (2,300 feet) deep and garlanded with cliffs and waterfalls, extends for 57 kilometres (35 miles). The peaks on the far side are the Three Rondavels ("Round Huts").

The Swadini Dam, hemmed in by forest and cliff in the bottom of the Blyde River Canyon, is a popular destination for holidaymakers from Johannesburg, anxious to get away from the city.

Massive dolomitic boulders line the cliff edge above the canyon. Beyond are the Three Rondavels and dim in the blue distance is the Lowveld.

Over thousands of years these potholes have been carved in the Blyde River's limestone bed by the erosive action of tumbling stones and sand.

A spectacular view from the rim of the canyon gouged down the Great Escarpment by the Blyde River, showing where it spills out into the Lowveld.

Above: At the Lisbon Falls, one of many in the Drakensberg Escarpment, the Lisbon River drops nearly 90 metres (300 feet) into a deep dark pool.

Opposite: The Lisbon Falls seen from a vantage point above. One of the more accessible falls, it has a picnic site nearby.

Above: In the 1870s Pilgrim's Rest was a rip-roaring mining town born after "Wheelbarrow" Patterson found gold. Today, preserved in its original state, it is a quiet resort.

Left: At God's Window, near Graskop ("Grassy Head"), the Drakensberg Escarpment plunges almost sheer from the cool plateau down to the hot Lowveld about 1,000 metres (3,280 feet) below, giving quite breathtaking views.

Northwest Province and Northern Cape

The western slope of South Africa is an area of strong colours and immense space. The vast blue sky is often flecked with cottony clouds which soften the sun's fierce heat, but bring little rain. The Kalahari and Namib deserts spill in from the north so that from the extreme Northwest to the Northern Cape coast the terrain harshens steadily from fertile farmland to dry plains and arid desert.

The region is rich in produce: crops, wool, mutton, karakul, beef and dairy goods. It also abounds in minerals: gold, chrome, lead, tin, iron and immense quantities of coal, manganese and platinum. And diamonds: Kimberley is here, where miners dug the biggest man-made hole on earth with pick and shovel to extract 14.5 million carats. Gems are still prised from volcanic pipes, sifted from coastal dunes and dredged from the sea bed.

It is rich, too, in history. In the Northern Cape long-gone Bushmen painted colourful animals on cave walls. Unknown people left thousands of engravings on stone.

Above: When the sparse spring rains fall, arid Namaqualand in the Northern Cape produces an explosion of colour.

Left: Were it not for the extraordinary desert-adapted plants, like the halfmens ("half human") and other succulents, most of the Richtersveld National Park would resemble the surface of the moon.

Then came European explorers who mined copper near Springbok over 300 years ago. Two of the many who have ventured to this land were missionary Robert Moffat of Kuruman and his son-in-law, David Livingstone, who set out from there on his African explorations.

In the 1800s migrant Afrikaners settled in the Northwest, clashed with blacks and created short-lived republics. Here, the shot was fired that launched the Boer War; Mafeking (now Mafikeng) endured its famous siege; and Baden-Powell started the Boy Scout movement. Mankind's "missing link" – Australopithecus africanus – was found here in 1924.

Above all, the region is rich in stunning spectacle. At one extreme a game reserve thrives in an extinct volcano, near a casino resort. At another is the unique Kalahari Gemsbok National Park of blazing red dunes, home to springbok that once migrated in devastating millions. The vast semi-desert is pocked with eye-searing salt pans, ridged by dunes or carpeted with quartz and garnet pebbles. Through this landscape the Orange River flows on its 2,340 kilometre (1,455 mile) course to the Atlantic through the 250 metre (820 foot) Augrabies Canyon and past the moonscape of the Richtersveld National Park.

To the south is the huge Great Karoo, studded with flat-top and sugarloaf mountains and full of dinosaur fossils. And in the far west is arid Namaqualand, where in good years nature briefly carpets the entire land in a wild flower display of unparalleled brilliance.

Opposite: Because of the dust in the air and cloud generated by the cold Atlantic ocean nearby, the Richtersveld Desert produces dramatic sunsets that paint the peaks with orange.

Below: The lonely gravel road to the mountainous Richtersveld on the Namibia border winds past brief spring flowers and stunted desert.

Everything in the Kalahari Gemsbok National Park appears with brilliant clarity, like the moon setting over the ancient, bright red sand dunes.

Above: Springbok can go for long periods without water but fill up when they can before setting off to browse in the Kalahari.

Opposite: South Africa's largest and longest river, the Orange, plunges 91 metres (300 feet) into an 18 kilometre (11 mile) solid rock ravine at the Augrabies Falls near Upington in the Northern Cape. In flood, it is one of the world's six largest falls.

Top: Suricates are a kind of mongoose living in the Kalahari, noted for their close-knit family life and extreme alertness. Here a mother and youngster do sentry duty.

Above: Wildebeest need water almost daily and make frequent use of the artificial waterholes in the Kalahari Gemsbok National Park.

Left: Though mostly waterless, the Kalahari is not a true desert and has great park-like plains with camel-thorn trees. Here a herd of blue wildebeest trek to water.

Left: Bat-eared fox and cub play in the dust in the Kalahari.

Below: The flat, barren landscape, with only one shrub visible, in the lonely emptiness of the Richtersveld.

Opposite: Thousands of men wielding picks and shovels dug this, the largest man-made hole in the world, to extract 14.5 million carats of diamonds at Kimberley. The mine closed in 1914 and water half-fills the hole but the city remains the capital of the Northern Cape.

Above: Rural scene of the original school house, still standing at the Moffat Mission at Kuruman.

Right: When Namaqualand bedecks itself with new floral clothing, it attracts thousands of tourists worldwide. Here, merino sheep relish the rich pasture.

Opposite: Morning sun silvers the Orange River in the great gorge below the Augrabies Falls. In flood the river has filled the gorge to the brim.

Left: A cluster of halfmens ("half human") succulent trees stand solemn guard beside the Orange River where it forms the border between the Northern Cape and Namibia on the far side.

Below: Rock lobster fishermen's dinghies at Hondeklip ("Dog Rock") Bay on the desert coast of the Northern Cape. The little port is used by the sea diamond dredging industry.

Bottom: A Topnaar woman of Khoi descent preparing a Dutch oven for baking. Such wood-fuelled clay ovens have been in use for centuries.

This strange tree in the starkly dramatic scenery of the Hester Malan Nature Reserve in Namaqualand is called a kokerboom or "quiver tree" because Bushmen made quivers from its bark.

For a few weeks a year, yellow spring flowers in Namaqualand blaze with a brilliance that draws people from all over the world.

The stunning red blooms of the Jakkalsblam plant ("jackal flowers") cover the red earth of Namaqualand.

A contrast in colours: two kinds of daisies among the 4,000 species of wild flowers that annually transform great areas of barren Namaqualand into a place of rare beauty.

A woman of the Topnaar, some of the last surviving Khoi people, sits proudly on the steps of her brick house wearing an old-style bonnet against the fierce sun.

A typical homestead, with its windpump and outbuildings, nestles between Namaqualand hills, an oasis in the desert.

Above: The Lost City, an extravagantly luxurious hotel and casino resort in the wilds of the Northwest Province, is the product of the extraordinary vision of a South African hotelier.

Left: No expense was spared to create the wide variety of attractions at the Lost City such as the highly popular Waterworld, with a host of imported vegetation.

Opposite: The façade of the Lost City: a mélange of African and Eastern design topped with elephant tusk cupolas. This resort and two ancillary casinos draw hundreds of thousands of visitors annually.

Above left: The soaring main foyer of the Lost City is graced by this statue of the famous giant Kruger National Park elephant, Shawu.

Above right: The Waterworld has its own artificial shore and beach. All the materials had to be brought from elsewhere.

Above: The Rustenburg Nature Reserve lies at the western edge of South Africa's temperate zone before it steadily gives way to increasingly arid country.

Right: The donkey-drawn cart is a common and cheap means of transport for the people of the Northern Cape, and a good way to enjoy the flowers lining the roadside.

Opposite: A gentle series of waterfalls cascades through the hilly country around Rustenburg in the Northwest Province.

Gauteng

The Gauteng (Sotho for "Place of Gold") is a province of superlatives. It is the smallest, with only 17,010 square kilometres (6,570 square miles) but is home to between seven and eight million people, second only to the far larger KwaZulu/Natal. It is South Africa's economic capital with the biggest output, payroll, buildings, fortunes and crime rate. It lives at a frenetic pace.

It contains a string of cities, most born during the hectic 1886 gold rush when the world's largest deposits were found on the Witwatersrand ("Ridge of White Waters"). Most have virtually fused into one huge conurbation, a long east-west string of highways, railroads, downtowns, factories, suburbs, malls, stadia and slums, beaded with ugly mine dumps and tailings dams. Largest are

Above: Modern Johannesburg architecture – a tall tangle of angles and curves in bleak steel, glass and concrete, reflecting money and conflicting tastes. It is said that buildings are torn down when they are twenty years old to make way for the new.

Left: Central Johannesburg, business hub of South Africa and of Gauteng, is the most crowded and polyglot metropolitan area in all Africa after Cairo. In the foreground is the densely populated high-rise Hillbrow flatland and, beyond it, the mini-Chicago of downtown.

Johannesburg, its apartheid-born "twin city" Soweto (SOuth WEstern TOwnships), Pretoria, the architecturally impressive administrative capital, the new city of Midrand, and the Vereeniging industrial complex.

In Johannesburg making and minding money is everybody's business, from magnates in their penthouses to the masses haggling on the sidewalks below. Its downtown is a mini-Chicago of vertical concrete and glass – hectic by day, hazardous by night; its leafy suburbs are green seas islanded with malls; it is rimmed by squatter camps and townships. Most of its fellow cities are similar, but on a lesser scale.

Yet Gauteng is far from soulless. It froths with life. Social change has made it a spicy stew of every race, creed, language, colour and custom. Many theatres, museums and gardens, together with hundreds of restaurants and markets, provide entertainment and intellectual stimulus. Two of the world's leading zoological gardens are here. It is home to four universities. Its musical and theatrical events attract top international performers. It hosts international sports matches. It has beautiful parks, sanctuaries and hiking trails. It contains valuable archaeological sites.

It offers something for everyone, a hub for brains and beauty as well as money. It is the hard-beating heart of South Africa.

Opposite top: Sculpted bird souvenirs are included in an array of arts and crafts on sale at Johannesburg's highly popular Bruma Lake flea market, held every weekend.

Opposite middle: The streets around the huge Carlton shopping centre and hotel in central Johannesburg are an incessant stream of people of every race and colour, selling, buying or patronizing the many restaurants, cafés, cinemas and other entertainment venues.

Opposite bottom: The fairyland brilliance of Johannesburg's lights hides a harsh night world of poverty and crime. The brightest and tallest is the Hillbrow broadcasting tower.

Above: In October many of Johannesburg's streets and gardens are filled with the lilac-blue of jacaranda trees in bloom. Imported from Brazil, these trees are prized in cities but have become an invasive pest in the countryside.

Middle right: Rocky Street is an old part of Johannesburg with an eclectic mix of pubs, clubs, the heavy beat of pop and experimental music, way-out clothing, junk and pawn shops, drugs and a hectic night-life.

Right: The elaborately decorated entrance to a Chinese restaurant contrasts quaintly with an African medicine shop on one side and the barred door of an anonymous business on the other. Johannesburg has many Oriental eating places.

Top: The huge Ellis Park rugby stadium in Johannesburg was built in 1982 and is seen here filled to capacity for a big game. The change to democracy put South Africa in the forefront of world rugby.

Above: The Johannesburg Stock Exchange's modern home, where fortunes change hands daily, mainly in local mining and industrial shares. Founded in 1887, it is comparatively small by international standards, but is now attracting more foreign interest.

Right: A panorama of Johannesburg's central business district reveals many old, smaller buildings crowded at the feet of its semi-skyscrapers. The new trend is to preserve the best of the old.

When the Rugby World Cup Final was played at Ellis Park stadium in 1995 it was preceded by exhibitions of national cultures, including these energetic, befeathered tribal dancers. It worked: South Africa won.

Above: Sunset reflects off the glittering glass roof of a building in central Johannesburg so high and steep that young mountaineers from the Witwatersrand University are hired to clean it.

Left: Since the demise of apartheid thousands of black entrepeneurs have set up shop on Johannesburg's sidewalks where one can buy almost anything, including African masks for hanging on walls.

Johannesburg shoppers are increasingly served by huge malls where they can do all their buying under one roof. Four of the largest are named for the points of the compass, like Southgate in the southern suburbs.

Dwarfed by the tall blocks around it, the Johannesburg Art Gallery mainly exhibits the works of South African artists, but also has some valuable paintings and sculptures by great European artists.

Close to its overwhelming concentration of big buildings and busy streets, Johannesburg preserves slices of the original Witwatersrand, much as it was before the gold rush over a century ago. A walking trail along Linksfield Ridge gives a splendid view of the city skyline.

Left: At the new mushrooming city of Midrand, halfway between Johannesburg and Pretoria, birdwatchers find peace and quiet in a timbered hide in the Beaulieu bird sanctuary.

Below: A few miles outside Johannesburg, in the tranquil Highveld grasslands where cosmos blooms in the autumn, the throbbing city life seems light years away.

Opposite: A huge network of high-speed highways patterns Gauteng like a spider's web to link its many cities and towns. This one sweeping across farmland is between Pretoria and Krugersdorp.

Opposite bottom left: The long Magaliesberg range of mountains between Northwest Province and Pretoria in Gauteng is a favourite place for city people to escape to nature on its many trails and climbs. It has abundant wildlife.

Opposite bottom right: An old abandoned gold-mine headgear and works on the outskirts of Johannesburg. The Witwatersrand is cluttered with them and with dumps and dams.

Above: Tree-lined Pretoria, South Africa's administrative capital, 50 kilometres (30 miles) north of Johannesburg, is known for its blend of old and new architecture. This view is of office and apartment blocks on the edge of the city centre.

Right: High-rise buildings in Pretoria's city centre, seen from the terraced gardens of the Union Buildings, project above its afternoon layer of haze.

Opposite: One of the favourite centres of diversion for Gauteng's landlocked residents is an entire waterfront shopping and entertainment complex constructed in Randburg City on Johannesburg's northern side.

Above: Pretoria is famed for its avenues of jacaranda trees which turn the streets bright lilac-blue for a month or two from September every year, spreading carpets of blossom on the sidewalks.

Right: The squat stone bulk of the Voortrekker Monument was built on a hilltop outside Pretoria between 1938 and 1949 to commemorate the trials and tribulations of the Afrikaner pioneers who came from the Cape in ox-wagons.

The Union Buildings in Arcadia, Pretoria, one of Sir Herbert Baker's most gracious designs, were erected to mark the formation of the Union of South Africa in 1910. The edifice used to accommodate the entire government but now houses only the Presidential and Foreign Affairs offices.

Above: Women of the Ndebele tribe near Pretoria, part of the Nguni group which includes the Zulu, take great pride in decorating the walls of their houses and gardens in dazzling colours, which are repeated in their dress.

Right: An Ndebele woman threading beads on string wears the bright headdress, blanket and brass collars typical of her people. They also wear many brass bracelets and anklets.

Above: Major efforts are under way to improve the quality of life in the "informal settlements" or squatter camps around Gauteng's cities and, in the process, to provide employment for many people.

Right: Part of the vast sprawl of Soweto (South Western Townships). The collection of some 18 townships, created by the former regime as a black dormitory and labour reservoir for Johannesburg, has developed a momentum and character of its own and, although apartheid has gone, it remains home to at least two million people. Some parts have middle- to upper-class homes, and the little box houses visible here are slowly being upgraded.

Above: Middle class housing in the Soweto Pimville township.

Left: Gold Reef City on Johannesburg's southern edge is a reconstruction of the city in its early days, complete with hotel, museums, brewery, steam train, saloons and dancing girls, all on the site of the Crown Mine, the world's richest until it closed in 1975.

Below: The Vaal ("Pale") River flowing at the southern end of Gauteng is the province's most important source of water. It is already inadequate, however, so a huge dam project has begun to feed in water from the highlands of landlocked Lesotho far to the south.

Opposite: Cities, industries and agriculture all place a huge demand on the Vaal River, seen here flowing in southern Gauteng. It is also heavily used for water sports.

KwaZulu/Natal

KwaZulu/Natal – named Terra dos Fumos ("Land of Smoke") by Portuguese navigators for its bushfires – is a scenic paradise drenched in the blood of past wars. History has dealt harshly here. Two centuries ago Shaka ruthlessly welded the Zulus into one nation in turmoil that rocked all southern Africa. Then the Zulus fought the British and Afrikaners who, after subduing them, fought each other.

The fighting in all these wars left a string of bloodied battlefields across the whole province: some famous like Isandlwana where Zulus trounced the British; Rorke's Drift where 11 brave men earned Victoria Crosses; and Colenso and Spioenkop, where the Boers defeated the British.

Today the nine million people of this 92,100 square kilometre (35,560 square mile) province live amicably, except for periodic isolated violence between Zulu clans and political groups. Some three-quarters of the people are Zulu and the rest are a zesty spicing of Hindu, Muslim, English, Afrikaner and mixed-race.

The province is South Africans' favourite holiday destination. Hemmed between the Indian Ocean and the Drakensberg Escarpment, the terrain changes swiftly from tropical beaches to Alpine heights reaching 3,376 metres (11,075 feet) and offers a multitude of attractions: superb game reserves teeming with wildlife, dense primordial forests, long vistas of tumbled hills, balmy savannah and the emerald foothills below the spectacular walls of the Drakensberg, where Bushmen long ago filled the walls of many caves with colourful paintings. Many rivers rising in the heights cross the region through deep valleys and gorges. In the north, behind gold-yellow beaches fringed by coral, are huge shallow lagoons populated by thousands of crocodile, hundreds of hippo and millions of birds.

Left: Creamy rollers of the warm Indian Ocean break idly on the long golden beach of Kosi Bay in the far north of KwaZulu/Natal: a paradise of tropical marine life.

KwaZulu/Natal is full of picturesque towns and villages, trout fishing lodges and resorts – more than 50 of them dotted along the coast – scores of museums and monuments, Zulu kraals, churches, temples and mosques. Mahatma Gandhi developed his philosophy here. The last Napoleon, Louis, died in battle here.

The main centre is Durban, Africa's largest port and a glittering Mecca for tourists. Next is Pietermaritzburg, 90 km (56 miles) inland – a gracious Victorian city that was for long the provincial capital.

Below: The Mkuzi Game Reserve, inland in northern KwaZulu/Natal, hosts a great variety of birds, antelope and predators and also a forest of huge sycamore fig trees which provide a haven and food for many creatures.

Opposite: The tall sycamore fig trees with their flying buttress roots, big leaves and fruits sprouting directly from the bark are a water-loving species and create shadowed canopies on river banks.

Above: The Hluhluwe River, named after a thorny creeper, is one of many crossing KwaZulu/Natal. It runs through the 230 square kilometre (88 square mile) Hluhluwe Game Reserve with magnificent tropical forest and many animals including lion, rhino and elephant.

Left: Lesser kudu graze on the grassy bank of the Hluhluwe River, shaded by spreading thorn trees, while a flotilla of wild duck make their way to the water.

Opposite above: An important feature of KwaZulu/Natal's parks is the involvement of local communities. These Zulu dancers are performing at the Dumazulu cultural village in the Hluhluwe reserve, dressed in the sort of finery British forces saw in the 19th-century Zulu wars.

Opposite below: Wide-lipped white rhino sport on a river bank in the evening before drinking. Hluhluwe and its sister reserve, Umfolozi, are where the white rhino were saved from extinction by the dedication of a handful of rangers.

Left: These golden dunes at Cape Vidal are part of the large St Lucia Game Reserve on the northern KwaZulu/Natal coast. A huge public outcry recently persuaded the government to ban a project to mine the ancient coastal dunes in this ecologically sensitive area.

Below: St Lucia comprises four reserves around a great, shallow estuarine lake, populated by thousands of crocodiles and hippos and a vast variety of water-birds. This view is of sunrise on Lake St Lucia looking towards Cape Vidal.

Opposite above: Waterbuck, one of the many species in the Umfolozi Game Reserve, make a frieze against the shallow water of the Umfolozi River, glittering in the late afternoon sun.

Opposite below: Northern KwaZulu/Natal is a never-ending display of superb scenery. Here the rising sun picks out the hills and trees of Umfolozi in delicate shades of pastel.

Above: Durban, Africa's largest port and one of the biggest in the southern hemisphere. Founded in 1835 and named after Sir Benjamin D'Urban, Governor of the Cape Colony, it is a vibrant, kaleidoscopic city of Europeans, Africans and Indians. The fine natural harbour accommodates ships of any size and handles huge volumes of container and other traffic mostly for the inland provinces, particularly Gauteng.

Right: A forest of high-rise buildings in Durban's central business district overlooks the yacht basin and harbour. In the foreground is an example of the older colonial style of buildings, many of which have been restored.

Above: The Durban beachfront, lined with skyscraper hotels like an African Miami, is the most popular seaside venue in South Africa and is crammed with hedonists on holiday. It is a centre for international surfing contests and offers many kinds of entertainment including, for the daring, bunjee jumping.

Left: A sight to delight the seafood lover: crabs galore in the Victoria Street Market where Indian traders and their customers haggle noisily over all kinds of produce, including seafood and spices.

Left: Pietermaritzburg, KwaZulu/Natal's long-time capital, 90 kilometres (56 miles) inland from Durban, was founded by Afrikaner pioneers who formed a small republic there. But after Britain colonized Natal it evolved into a typically Victorian town with features like this bandstand at the Alexandra Park cricket oval.

Below: Pietermaritzburg's fine old city hall reflects the architectural styles of the colonial heyday. Built in 1893, it is said to be the biggest brick building in the southern hemisphere. It was destroyed by fire in 1898 and rebuilt three years later.

Opposite above: The place where these lion cubs are playing is the Phinda Resource Reserve: founded by a private game reserve company to develop tourism for the benefit of the local black communities in the north of KwaZulu/Natal.

Opposite below: In the Kokstad area, in the far south of KwaZulu/Natal, sunflowers are one of the regular crops. The seed has a high oil content. The area is known mainly for its cattle ranching and horse breeding.

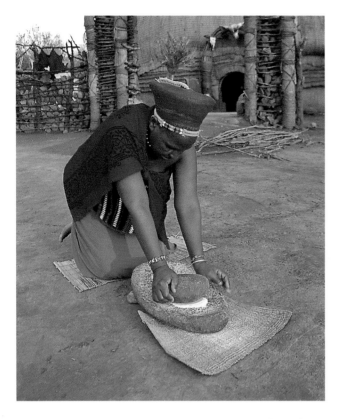

For thousands of years African women have ground their millet, and now their maize, as this Zulu woman is doing outside her beehive hut. The corn is placed on the large stone and crushed with the smaller one in a pushing motion.

This elderly Zulu is fashioning a knobkerrie, the traditional long-hafted club Zulu men carry about with them as familiarly as Englishmen used to carry walking-sticks. Leaning against the hut wall behind him are two throwing spears.

Pretty young Zulu women pose outside a hut in Shakaland, a "living museum" where Zulu customs are demonstrated. Carrying their water pots on their heads, they walk with great grace. Their dresses are an adopted style but their headbands are traditional.

A Zulu warrior greets the sunrise over his domain much as his forefathers must have done when Europeans encountered them nearly 200 years ago, shield in one hand, short stabbing spear in the other.

The Zulu bride on the left partly conceals her face behind a curtain and wears the platform headdress of a wife. The girl on the right hides her face because she is betrothed.

At Mdukutshani in the overcrowded Msinga region of KwaZulu/Natal, dedicated people are encouraging Zulus to grow more and better crops to feed themselves, like the plump maize cobs this boy is holding.

Newly hatched loggerhead turtles extricate themselves from the sandy nest their mother dug on a beach in northern KwaZulu/Natal, and instinctively head straight for the sea. Most will be eaten by predators, but the survivors will grow to about 150 kilograms (330 pounds). Up to 500 females lay eggs on these beaches every year.

In the southern winter the magnificence of the Drakensberg Mountains, soaring to over 3,000 metres (more than 10,000 feet) above sea level, is enhanced by a cloak of snow, sometimes light, sometimes very deep.

At the northern end of the highest part of the Drakensberg is a series of cliffs and peaks called the Amphitheatre. To climb one peak, the Sentinel, hikers must use this precarious-looking chain ladder.

The Amphitheatre is the great curve of soaring cliffs in the background, bracketed by high peaks. One of the most awesome spectacles in Africa, it is in a park rich in wildlife and is the source of eight rivers.

Cattle graze on the cool lower slopes of the Drakensberg near the Injabuti hut camp beneath the heights of the Giant's Castle Nature Reserve. The "'Berg", as locals call it, has good amenities for people tackling its tough hikes and climbs.

Above: In the Cathkin Peak sector of the Drakensberg a steep dark prominence called the Monk's Cowl rises from the rim of the Escarpment to 3,234 metres (10,610 feet) above sea level. Mountaineers treat it with great wariness because it has a treacherous reputation.

Opposite: The Drakensberg is festooned with waterfalls tumbling down to become the rivers that cut across KwaZulu/Natal to the Indian Ocean. This one, in the Giant's Castle Reserve, is one of the lesser falls.

Superb Sodwana Bay National Park, in northern KwaZulu/Natal, is a gathering place for scuba divers and for surf fishermen who in certain parts are allowed to drive four-wheel-drive vehicles on to the beach to launch their ski-boats.

Above: Most of its trains are powered by electricity or diesel, but South Africa still has a number of standard and narrow gauge steam trains that draw buffs from all over the world, such as the Banana Express between Port Shepstone and Harding.

Opposite: Where the rivers crossing KwaZulu/Natal meet the warm sea along the south coast, many are barred by sand dunes and form lagoons which are idyllic settings for holiday resorts, making this coastal region one of South Africa's top vacation destinations.

Free State

Many travellers through this 129,480 square kilometre (49,990 square mile) province are daunted by the dreariness of its monotonous savannah. Those who look further discover a great store of history, beauty and activity.

It is very old. The world's largest dinosaur roamed it 200 million years ago. It saw a pageant of peoples: prehistoric man, early Stone Age and Iron Age man; unknown people who painted on rock in distinctive style; Bushmen who filled hundreds of caves and crevices with brilliant

Above: The very distinctive facial profile of this cliff is called Gladstone's Nose, a name probably given by British troops camped in this part of the Free State during the Boer War.

Left: The giant sandstone buttresses rising loftily from eroded green slopes give the Golden Gate Highlands National Park in the north-east Free State its name: the light of the setting sun turns them gold-yellow. They are part of the geological tumble which makes up the Drakensberg Escarpment and the Maluti Mountains. Beneath them is the Little Caledon River.

polychrome paintings; warring black armies in the 18th and 19th centuries; Afrikaners who came with horses and wagons, set up a model republic and fought the Basotho people; British troops who promptly annexed the republic, gave it back, then took it again.

The Boer War swathed the Free State in battlefields and monuments and, saddest of all, the graves of thousands of Boer women and children who died in prisoner-of-war camps. Today its 2.8 million people live in unusual amity.

Late in the 19th century diamonds were discovered, among them the huge Excelsior of 971 carats and the pure white Reitz of 637 carats. Now, in the area around Welkom, the province produces about half of South Africa's gold. At Sasolburg it boasts the first viable oil-from-coal plant. Its farms produce most of the nation's maize as well as wheat, sorghum, sunflower seed, wool, mutton, beef and – at picturesque Ficksburg – cherries.

The north and east, far from being flat and dull, contain some of South Africa's most singularly beautiful scenery. The savannah gives way to the magnificent ridges and slopes of the Maluti Mountains, rising eastward to the Drakensberg pinnacles overlooking KwaZulu/Natal. Here, near the little artists' village of Clarens, is the Golden Gate Highlands National Park, named for the brilliant colour of its giant sandstone bluffs.

The capital Bloemfontein, the "Flower Fountain" – a pretty, conservative city of gracious old and garish new buildings – is also the nation's judicial capital and the crossroads to everywhere.

Below: The Little Caledon flows quietly past one of the many vertical sandstone bluffs in the Golden Gate Highlands National Park. Dinosaur fossils have been found here and the area was favoured by the Bushman people for its many caves and abundant water and game.

Above: The steep mountain slopes of the Golden Gate National Park are the habitat of oribi, eland, blesbok, springbok, reebok and black wildebeest. In most winters the scene is blanketed by snow.

Below: The headquarters and main accommodation at Golden Gate is the luxurious Brandwag ("Sentry") Lodge at the foot of a tall yellow buttress named the Sentinel.

Above: Early winter turns the poplars russet on the road between the little artists' village of Clarens and the Golden Gate park, a scene typical of the eastern fringes of the Free State.

Left: Basotho farmworkers in the Clarens district live in solidly built mud-walled houses with thick thatched roofs to ward off the bitter cold of winter, when clothes left on the washing line tend to freeze.

Opposite above and below left: Yellowing poplars make a pretty, placid late-afternoon scene in autumn on a small farm near Clarens, reminiscent of parts of New England. Peaceful now, the area has seen two wars, the Boer War and the conflict of 1866 in which Transvaal President Paul Kruger led a campaign against the Basotho people. The district was named after the Swiss village where he died in exile.

Opposite below right: Sheep are one of the farm animals better able to withstand the fiercely cold winters of the north-east Free State, which is sometimes cut off by snow and iced roads.

Above: Flat-topped mountains crowned by cliffs, like this one near Harrismith in the eastern Free State, are common all over the province and nearby Karoo and are the eroded remains of ancient plains.

Opposite: Harrismith, named after Cape Colony governor Sir Harry Smith, was founded at his order in 1850 to enable Britain to assert its authority over the area and guard against intrusion by the Afrikaner settlers. It is mainly a farming centre.

Overleaf: The meandering Vaal ("Pale") River is the vital artery of Gauteng province and the northern Free State. It forms their border and also that between the Free State and two other neighbours, the Northwest and Northern Cape, on its long journey from Mpumalanga, where it rises, to the Orange River.

Opposite above: They do not have the sea, say Free Staters, but the enormous sky compensates for it scenically. Here cotton-wool clouds decorate a landscape near Ficksburg in the east.

Opposite below: In Wagnerian mood, heavy storm clouds loom over a lonely old farmhouse in the Brandfort district, precursor to the curtains of rain coming from beyond.

Left: The peaceful city of Bloemfontein ("Flower Fountain"), capital of the Free State and judicial capital of South Africa, sprawls on the plains below Naval Hill, so named because British forces positioned naval guns here during the Boer War.

Below: The Appeal Court in Bloemfontein is South Africa's highest court of justice. It is one of many old buildings gracing the city, which grew from a watering-place for wagon trekkers in the early 19th century.

Above: The Sand River passes through the 105 square kilometre (40 square mile) Willem Pretorius Game Reserve in the western Free State. Created primarily to protect the black wildebeest, the reserve now has more than 700 other antelope of most species, and first-class amenities for visitors.

Opposite above: A resort much favoured by Free Staters and passing motorists is the Aventura Midwaters on the shore of the huge lake created by the Gariep Dam in the Orange River. It has excellent chalets, fishing and boating.

Opposite below: The resort has been designed for family holidays, with many amenities for young as well as old, such as its large swimming-pool, miniature golf, tennis and other sports facilities.

Above: The Eye of Zastron, a 9 metre (30 foot) hole in the Aasvoëlberg ("Vulture Mountain") above the town of Bethulie in the south-east Free State, has many legends. The favourite is that the Devil thought a farmer's muzzle-loader was a pipe, asked to smoke it and put the muzzle in his mouth. The farmer pulled the trigger and the Devil's head flew off and punched a hole in the rock, saying, "Phew, that's strong tobacco!"

Right: The lovely Orange River lily or *Crinumbulbispermum*, one of South Africa's many wild flowers, is the floral emblem of the Free State and ranges in colour from white to pink.

Opposite: The gracious old Dutch Reformed Church (DRC) at Bethulie ("Chosen by God") next to the Gariep Dam was completed in 1887 and is a national monument. Its clean white lines and silvered steeple are typical of DRC architecture of the time.

Top: A characteristic of the Free State is its sense of vast open space, shown in these dramatic pictures. Here the vastness is magnified by the thin vapour trail of an airliner passing in the far distance.

Above: A sunrise over the empty veld paints the clouds a gentle pink against the crisp blue of the sky.

Opposite: So absolutely clear is the Free State air that the lambent light of the setting sun picks out every tiny detail of the wide open landscape, down to the radio mast on the low ridge in the distance.

Western Cape

No other province has quite the diversity and grandeur of this one, enriched by its inhabitants and mellowed by time – the birthplace of South Africa.

When the Dutch settlers arrived in 1652, followed by French, Germans, English, Malays, Indonesians and Indians, the land was occupied by the Khoi and San peoples. They have gone but their cultures and genes are blended into the current population of some four million, living in 129,370 square kilometres (49,937 square miles).

All the facets of the region are visible in the mother city nestling in the lap of famous Table Mountain and in the necklace of suburbs, villages, harbours, wine estates and squatter settlements around the long narrow Cape Peninsula – the "Cape of Good Hope".

Above: Blue sea laps one of the many white beaches that surround the Cape Peninsula like a string of pearls.

Left: Created in 1913, the breathtaking Kirstenbosch Gardens on the eastern slopes of Table Mountain are famous for their incredible diversity of flowers. The 8 square kilometres (about 3 square miles), less than a tenth of it cultivated, contain some 5,000 species – nearly half of the Cape Peninsula's and a quarter of South Africa's, among them ericas, proteas, mesembryanthemums and aloes – and a priceless herbarium.

The province's terrain varies greatly from exuberant sub-tropical in the east to bleak semi-desert in the west and Karoo plains in the north. To the east is the Garden Route where the passing warmth of the Indian Ocean generates verdant growth between the sea and the ancient folded mountains inland. Its lakes, towns, bays, orchards and dense forests are a prime holiday attraction. One resort, Knysna, was developed by George Rex, reputedly the illegitimate son of King George III and Hannah Lightfoot. At another, Oudtshoorn, huge fortunes were made from ostrich feathers until fashion abandoned them.

From Mossel Bay, centre for offshore oil production, rolling wheatlands stretch westwards to Cape Agulhas, where the Atlantic and Indian Oceans meet and have wrecked many ships.

Nearer Cape Town are extensive apple orchards and endless vineyards surrounding elegant old gabled homesteads, source of the renowned Cape wines, against striking mountain backdrops. In the north-east the land rises through many valleys, some full of fruit in summer and snow in winter, to the bare Karoo.

From Cape Town the coastline turns north past great tracts of wheat into semi-desert. This is the fish-rich West Coast of blazing summers, chill winters and quaint customs. At giant Saldanha Bay, where the longest trains in the world deliver iron ore from inland, is the grave of Simeon Cummings, a crewman of the Confederate raider Alabama killed in a hunting accident. Further north the Western Cape joins the Northern Cape in a seasonal explosion of wild flowers.

The host of different environments supports many lifestyles. Relaxed Cape Town, the legislative capital, is the base for leading financial houses and some industry. Its superbly restored Victoria and Alfred Waterfront has a fantastic oceanarium for research and education. Home to many schools and universities, the province also has a multitude of museums, historical monuments, wine tours, scenic drives and trails, rock climbs, health spas, resorts and recreations involving the sea – especially game fishing and yachting. The escapades of its polyglot society are permanently entertaining. Basically dry in summer, wet in winter, its climate is highly changeable – it is, after all, the "Cape of Storms".

Nature has endowed it abundantly. With more than 8,600 plant species it is one of the world's six major floral kingdoms. The Kirstenbosch Gardens in Cape Town are as famous among botanists as Kew.

It has specialized game parks and reserves, dozens of mountain passes, fine beaches (though the sea is cold), beautiful towns and hamlets, and history under every step.

It is, as any Capetonian will say, the only place to be.

Below: An evening view over Cape Town city, the harbour and Table Bay.

Opposite, clockwise from top left: Cape Town University beneath towering Devil's Peak; a street in Bo-Kaap ("above Cape") suburb, home of the Malay community; the Greenmarket Square flea market in the heart of Cape Town, with Table Mountain and its "tablecloth" beyond; the Cecil Rhodes memorial on the east slope of Devil's Peak; an old church on Robben Island; the entrance to the superbly restored Victoria and Alfred Waterfront.

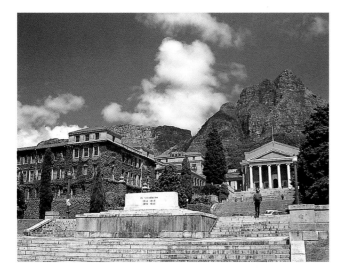

Above: The city buildings clinging to the land between Table Mountain and the Atlantic glitter white in the sharp rays of the sun. In the foreground is Blouberg Strand ("Blue Mountain Beach") across Table Bay.

Left: One of the most famous sights in the world and a navigator's landmark since the 15th century – an evening view of majestic Table Mountain rising to 1,086 metres (3,564 feet) above the sea with Devil's Peak on the left and Signal Hill and Lion's Head on the right.

Above: The Paarl ("Pearl") Rock high above the town of Paarl inland from Cape Town. The heart of the Cape wine industry, it was given that name because the rock shines like a pearl in the sun.

Above: They used to be known as jackass penguins because of their braying call but are now simply called South African penguins. These are on Jutten Island in the West Coast National Park.

Right: An aerial view of part of the 180 square kilometre (70 square mile) West Coast National Park comprising huge marshes, mudflats, plains and four islands around Saldanha Bay's Langebaan Lagoon. One of the finest wetlands in the world, it is home or a seasonal breeding-ground for nearly a million birds, including about 60,000 from the Arctic Circle.

Above: A picturesque farmhouse in the Swellendam district east of Cape Town, settled in 1745 and today a quiet, prosperous sheep and wheat farming district. Beyond are the folded mountains of the Western Cape.

Left: An aerial view of the enormously long "17 Mile Beach" at Langebaan Lagoon inside the huge Saldanha Bay on the West Coast.

Opposite above: Aloes put on a floral show against a backdrop of the folded mountains in the wilderness near Oudtshoorn, ostrich-farming capital of the Cape.

Opposite below: Mimosa Lodge is one of the grandiose country houses built about 1900 when Oudtshoorn's ostrich farmers made fortunes from the exclusive production of feathers for Europe's fashion houses. The fortunes collapsed with the fashion.

Above: With a small boy for audience, nature demonstrates its ephemeral artistry with evening colours over the Knysna Lagoon on the Garden Route.

Opposite above: The Garden Route along the southern edge of Africa provides panoramic views of the mingling Indian and Atlantic Ocean currents pounding the shore below steep cliffs.

Opposite below: The Wilderness is a long playground of lakes, lagoons, estuaries, verdant countryside and resorts on the Western Cape's south coast, known as the Lake District and renowned for its beauty.

Above: The Outeniqua Choo-Tjoe makes a scenic daily trip along the Garden Route from George to Knysna, where it swings across the big lagoon to enter the town before starting the journey back.

Left: In the Knynsa vicinity of the Garden Route, the benign climate encourages the rampant growth of forest and creeper. The freshwater streams interlacing the region supply a thriving timber and boat-building industry.

Above: The Union Jack and the new and old South African flags flutter together over a street stall in the pretty town of George, a largely English community at the western end of the Garden Route.

The beautiful beach and safe, warm water of Plettenberg Bay on the Garden Route are so popular with people of Gauteng province that it has been described as a long-distance suburb of Johannesburg.

The Beacon Island Hotel at Plettenberg Bay lights up like a Christmas tree at night. It is linked to the mainland by a bridge.

A street in Plettenberg Bay, which retains the character of a village in spite of its seasonal influx of thousands of wealthy inland visitors.

The enormous Cango Caves, extending deep into the Swartberg ("Black Mountains") near Oudtshoorn, are a series of dolomitic caverns filled with astounding limestone and crystalline forms created by the drip of lime-rich water over 100 million years.

Above: Sharp barren ridges rise from the Little Karoo viewed from the Seweweekspoort ("Seven Weeks Pass") through the Swartberg Mountains. Local legend says it took smugglers seven weeks to negotiate the pass.

Right: At 150-year-old Montagu in the Langeberg ("Long Mountain") Valley, inland from the Garden Route, are wine cellars, orchards and fine examples of Georgian and Cape Dutch architecture.

Opposite above: The new Karoo National Park near Beaufort West, in the north of the Western Cape, looks bleak but supports much wildlife and gives infinite vistas from the top of its craggy mountains.

Opposite below left: After the rains, grasses suddenly sprout and the stunted bushes turn green in the Karoo. This scene is at the Molteno Pass near Beaufort West.

Opposite below right: Sunlight on rain-laden air produces a great loop of rainbow over the Western Cape's Helderberg ("Bright Mountain").

The sea has a million moods on the Western Cape's multitude of shores. Here at Hermanus, east of Cape Town, it is layered with morning haze.

At Nature's Valley, east of Plettenberg Bay, gentle breakers caress the glistening beach on a calm summer's day.

Waves that look insignificant from the air smash on the feet of the craggy mountain peaks at the eastern tip of False Bay, encircled by the Cape Peninsula.

Not even the most daring of surfers risks these huge curling breakers thundering towards the rocks of the West Coast.

The Cape sea, which has sunk many ships, demonstrates its destructive power at the Storms River mouth.

Above: Wind and water have sculpted fantastic shapes, like the Wolfberg Arch, in the rock of the Cedarberg range between Citrusdal and Clanwilliam.

Right: Another strange sculpture is the Maltese Cross which seems to defy gravity on its precarious perch. The Cedarberg attracts many hikers and rock climbers and has a great variety of plants.

Opposite above: The Franschhoek ("French Corner") Valley, settled by Huguenot refugees near Cape Town almost 300 years ago, produces many of South Africa's finest French-styled wines from vineyards nestling below cloud-capped mountains.

Opposite below: An elderly steam train puffs through the Franschhoek Valley to show the sights to tourists riding in equally elderly coaches.

Eastern Cape

The place names give the hint to their origins: mainly melodious Xhosa in the east, English in the middle and Afrikaans in the west. They reflect the flux of people for over two centuries from the late 1700s when Afrikaners trekking east to escape the rule of Cape Town encountered Xhosa tribes. They clashed in 1779 and so began the nine Frontier Wars spanning the next century.

Britain annexed everything in 1806 and 14 years later sent 4,000 men, women and children in 21 ships to settle in and stabilize this distant African corner. They and their baggage were dumped on the beaches and left to contend with disease, drought, locusts, wild animals and hostile Xhosa.

Above: A smiling Xhosa matron in traditional black turban makes her way home from market carrying supper on her head. Xhosa women are renowned for the heavy loads they can carry this way.

Left: Human settlements on either side of the Umngazana River mouth in the Eastern Cape, where the warm Indian Ocean washes the remote, unspoiled Wild Coast, are dwarfed by the grandeur of the Transkei, mountainous home of the Xhosa people.

They were the 1820 Settlers, who gave South Africa a powerful infusion of English culture and skills and produced its first champions of the freedom of the Press.

The area they helped to tame stretches along the south-east coast between KwaZulu/Natal and the Western Cape. In its north, on the border with the tiny landlocked kingdom of Lesotho where the Drakensberg tails away, is some of South Africa's most spectacular mountain scenery. The countryside below is deeply notched by dizzying valleys, with rivers twisting far below through rocky gorges. This is the Transkei, heartland of the Xhosa, whose subtropical Wild Coast is little less wild than it was when Portuguese caravels were wrecked on it five centuries ago.

In the middle of this coast the 1820 Settlers made their homes, giving their settlements names redolent of their origins: East London, Port Elizabeth, Queenstown, Fort Beaufort, Alicedale. To the west, the southernmost reach of the Karoo brings its special character to places like Graaff-Reinet and Somerset East.

The province is 169,580 square kilometres (65,475 square miles) in area. East London is South Africa's fourth largest port and, with Port Elizabeth, serves a densely populated hinterland of some 7 million people. Grahamstown, a delightful city, is home to the important National Festival of the Arts every winter. Uitenhage is a centre for the automobile industry.

Above: The holiday chalets and homes of Presley's Bay nestle in the indigenous forest that grows in patches and pockets along the Wild Coast. It contains some unique plant and rare bird species. The coast is one of South Africa's best "get away from it all" vacation areas.

Right: The Wild Coast attracts sea anglers who cast their baits with long rods from the rocks and risk getting soaked by powerful waves surging from far out to crash on the shore.

Opposite: The Xhosa people like to build their mud-walled, thatch-roofed huts high on the slopes and ridges of the Transkei's tumbled landscape, where they till their fields, although it means long steep walks to fetch water from the rivers below.

Above: The Transkei is criss-crossed with rivers twisting their way from their catchments in the Drakensberg Mountains to the sea, many through deep gorges. They are the life blood of the Xhosa people and many, like the Mapuzi River emerging here near Coffee Bay, have holiday resorts near their estuaries.

Left: A view from the south of the Mapuzi estuary showing the rocky bar protecting it from the worst of the breakers and, beyond, the typically jumbled Transkei landscape.

Opposite: The Xhosa people living in these clusters of huts above the Mapuzi River enjoy some of the finest views in all Africa. At night they keep their livestock in the small kraals near their homes. They raise crops in small fields on the slopes.

Left: A typical Xhosa settlement near a small river winding tortuously to the sea near Coffee Bay. The villagers have built walls and grown hedges around their tilled lands to protect their crops from wild animals.

Below: A short distance south of Coffee Bay a great wall of bush-covered rock rises from the sea, a stone's throw from the shore. Right through the middle is a high, sea-carved arch known as the Hole in the Wall — probably the best-known natural oddity along the Wild Coast. Some of the Xhosa in this region are said to have in them the blood of sailors ship-wrecked centuries ago.

Opposite, clockwise from top: Pretty suburbs crowd the banks of the river at East London, founded in the 1840s to supply British garrisons protecting settlers against raiding Xhosa; the delightful Victorian town hall in East London, which services a huge inland population; customers of the restaurant in the city's Mpongo Park can watch geese browsing while they lunch; the Eastern Cape coast just north of East London is an endless succession of beaches, bays and lagoons.

Above: About halfway between East London and Port Elizabeth, Port Alfred is one of South Africa's leading coastal resorts. Founded as Port Frances by 1820 Settlers to supply the interior, it was renamed for Queen Victoria's son. It no longer serves as a harbour.

Left: A long stretch of wave-lapped beach on the scalloped coastline near Port Alfred is named Kleinmond ("Little Mouth") for the small river there, its exit blocked by sand.

Opposite above: For the lover of elephants there is no better place to study them than in the Addo section of the Addo/Zuurberg National Park near Port Elizabeth. Numbering nearly 200, they are the last of the Cape elephants and are descended from 11 individuals saved in 1919 after hunters had been hired to wipe out the herd to make way for farming.

Opposite below: The district of Elliot in the high Eastern Cape interior is ranching country known for its mushrooms and also for the extraordinary castellated peaks and pillars of the nearby Drakensberg. It was named after a British army officer who settled here in the 1880s.

These rugged hills and mist-filled valleys are in the Mountain Zebra National Park in the high Karoo, inland from Port Elizabeth. It was created in 1937 as a haven for the Cape mountain zebra, one of the world's rarest species. There are now more than 230 sharing the park with other buck and a variety of birds.

The thriving city of Port Elizabeth was founded by the 1820 Settlers and named by the British governor, Sir Rufane Donkin, after his young wife who had died two years earlier. South Africa's fifth largest harbour, it has been nicknamed the "Windy City" because of the easterlies that blow through it, but also the "Friendly City" for its hospitality and welcoming beaches.

Giant Outeniqua yellowwood trees, highly prized for making furniture but protected here, soar above the creeper canopy of the ancient indigenous Tsitsikamma Forest on the coast between Port Elizabeth and Knysna. Some of the trees are up to 800 years old and over 50 metres (165 feet) tall. The climate that produces this lush growth is generated by the meeting off this coast of the warm Indian Ocean and cold Atlantic Ocean currents.

The spectacularly deep and narrow gorge of the Storms River slices through the Tsitsikamma Forest to the sea. The area is protected by two parks, one of which extends 5 kilometres (3 miles) into the sea to preserve the abundant marine and shore life, including the Cape clawless otter and sea snakes.

Top: A young couple have a beach at Tsitsikamma to themselves in the late afternoon. Some of the country's most popular hiking trails are in this region, notably the Otter Trail along the shore.

Above: Clean cool streams and pools like this one emerging from the forest give welcome refreshment to people hiking the beautiful and extremely popular Otter Trail.

Top: Everything beneath the surface of the sea as well as above is preserved in Tsitsikamma National Park, the first marine park to be created in South Africa.

Above: The water is pure and drinkable, filtered by the forest, aerated by its swift passage over the rocks and cleaned by inhabitants such as crabs and frogs.

Above: A hiker on the Otter Trail pauses to savour the stunning blend of blue sea, white beach and verdant coastal hills near Tsitsikamma. So popular is this trail that reservations must be made a year in advance. Hikers spend the nights in simple but comfortable huts.

Left: One of the many highlights along this splendid coastline is the precarious-looking but perfectly safe Paul Sauer suspension bridge, 139 metres (450 feet) above the mouth of the Storms River, giving a view up the precipitous gorge.

Index

Picture Credits

All pictures courtesy of Anthony Bannister Picture Library (ABPL), South Africa.

Shaen Adey: p73b, p79b, p83bl, p84b, p109ml, p127b. Daryl Balfour: p12t, p56t, p75b, p126t. Andrew Bannister: p5m, p51r, p52t, p53t/m. Anthony Bannister: p1m, p2tl, p9, pp10-11, p12bl, p13, p22l, pp28-29, p29r, p33, p35t, pp36-37, p45tl, p46t, p47tr, p59bl, pp68-69, p82, p83br, p89r, p90, p91t/b, p104bl, p112l, pp112-113, p114b, p124b, p129r, p137t, p138t, p139, p140, p141tl/tr/bl. Barbara Bannister: p81br. Donald Barnett: p52m, p119br. Daphne Carew: p43tr. Pat de la Harpe: p74t, p108. Roger de la Harpe: p2 tr/br, p63t/b, p66t, p73t, p74b, p77b, p78b, p80tl/tr/b, p81t/bl, p84t, p85, p87b, p99t, p101t/b, 104tl, p109ml, pp110-111, p121. Nigel J. Dennis: p2ml, p12br, p14tl/bl, p16m, p17br, p19r, p37tr, p58b, p70, p83t, p100, p131b. Pat Donaldson: p1t. Thomas Dressler: p16b. Richard du Toit: p1b, p78t, p109tl, p111br. Aaron Fankental: p3m. Athol Franz: pp50-51, p54tl/bl, pp54-55, p58t, p60, p134b. p142t/b. Malcom Funston: pp18-19, p71. Clarke L. Gittens: p41t, p59t, p62tl. Clem Haagner: p41b, p44bl. Gerald Hinde: p124t. Luc Hosten: p4m. Luke Hunter: p79t. Kim Hutton: p5t, p46b. Peter Lillie: p38t. Tim Liversedge: p2bl. Robert Nunnington: p20b, p21, pp22-23, p24t/bl/br, p25, p26, p27, p34, p35b, p40, p72t, pp88-89. Rod Patterson: p37br. Rob Ponte: p92t/b. Herman Potgieter: pp6-7, p76t/b, p86, p87t, p94, 125t, pp128-129, p131t, p132t/b, p133, p134t, p135t,ml/ bl, 136t/b, 138b. Dewald Reiners: p4b, p8, p62tr/b, pp64-65, p67, p95, pp96-97, p103t, p109bl. Phillip Richardson: p2mr, p39. Brendan Ryan: p47b. Joan Ryder: p93t/bl/br. Wayne Saunders: p20t. Southlight: p64bl. Lorna Stanton: p14-15, p17t/bl, p48, p53b, p56bl, p57b, p75t, p98b, p122t/bl. Loretta Steyn: pp104-5. Guy Stubbs: p3b, p4t, p64tl, p72b, pp106-7, p109tr. Colla Swart: p31r, p38b, p43br, p44br, p45tr, p49b. Warwick Tarboton: 103b. Gavin Thomson: p5b, p16t. Lisa Trocchi: p47tl, p52b, p56br, p57tl/tr, p61b. Johan van Jaarsveld: p49t, p66b. Chris van Lennep: p77t, p107r, 125bl. Hein von Horsten: p3t, pp42-43, p44t, p59br, p61t, p98t, p102, p109br, p115t, p117, p119tr, p122br, p123b, p127t, p135bl, 137b. Lanz von Horsten: pp30-31, p32, p45b, p111tr, p114t, p115b, p116t/b, p118-119, p120t/ bl/br, p123t, p125br, p126b, p130, p135br, p141br.